The CAMRA Guide to

by Ted Bruning

Author: Ted Bruning

Published by CAMRA Books, Campaign for Real Ale, 230 Hatfield Road, St Albans AL1 4LW
Tel: 01727 867201 Fax: 01727 867670
Managing Editor: Mark Webb
Design/Layout and Cover Illustration: Mckie Associates
ISBN 1-85249-132-9

First Edition, September 1997

Great effort has gone into researching the contents of this book, but no responsibility can be taken for errors.

Front Cover: Harvey & Son's Bridge Wharf Brewery, Lewes, Sussex

Back Cover: Jennings' Castle Brewery, Cockermouth, Cumbria

CONTENTS

Visiting a Brewery

A few years ago it would have been hard to see breweries as tourist attractions.

There have always been school tours of factories, and visits could be arranged for industrial archeological societies and the like, but few people were interested in the brewing process as such, and they would be as likely to visit a coal-mine or a woollen-mill as a brewery.

Anyway, many breweries were grim Victorian industrial buildings which weren't thought terribly attractive, and the face which the average brewing company preferred to show the world was its tied pubs and its beer brands.

There are still traditionally-minded brewers who are grudging with tours and see visitors as bloody nuisances who only get in the way. In a sense, they're right: the more attractive country breweries such as Hook Norton in Oxfordshire would be swamped in an instant if tour parties were not strictly rationed.

For along with increasing public interest in real ale has come interest in the brewing process itself, while the Victorian industrial architecture which characterises so many breweries is back in favour.

And with so many beers being sold far from their breweries of origin, many brewers are anxious that as many people as possible should get to taste their ales in perfect condition – and that means in the sample room.

More and more, then, breweries are proving just as attractive to visitors as their satellite pubs.

Small brewers have been especially quick to see the advantage of attracting visitors. With no advertising budgets and few if any tied pubs, tours, visitors' centres, and counter-sales of bottled beer, branded glasses, sweatshirts and so on are a cost-effective means of promotion and can be profitable in themselves.

Many of these small breweries are housed in the outbuildings of coaching inns, converted farmyards, and other sites attractive enough to merit a visit in their own right. Some are even in stately homes.

Others, though, are more industrial in character, but have still found that the lure of beer and brewing is so strong that, given the addition of a licensed visitor centre, they have attracted tourists in appreciable numbers.

It's not only small brewers that have grasped the importance of welcoming the public through the brewery doors, though: many of the old-established regional firms have too.

In some cases these are cramped town-centre sites with few obvious charms, but in many cases they are enormously attractive destinations or, like Elgood's of Wisbech with its fabulous gardens, have decked themselves out to make as wide an appeal as possible.

But handsome or no, it's time that more breweries started making the most of their tourism potential.

For tourists, they say, always end up destroying what they have come to visit – but in this case at least, they couldn't be more wrong.

After all, would country breweries like Rayment's of Furneux Pelham, Hertfordshire, Wethered's of Marlow, Buckinghamshire, and Wem of Wem in Shropshire, have been axed quite so readily if they had had queues of tourists at their doors?

And would Fremlin's of Faversham in Kent still be with us if it, its neighbour Shepherd Neame, and some of the area's many hop gardens, had all been stops on some Kentish Oast Trail?

There are other sound campaigning reasons why CAMRA would like to encourage breweries to open their doors to the public:

• In brewery sample rooms, members of the public can taste real ales in peak condition – especially important in the era of guest ales, when beers may travel from depot to depot, often taking weeks to reach an unfamiliar pub far from the brewery, in uncertain condition. If your first taste of the best beer of the world is of a ruined travesty, you'll probably never try it again.

• Brewery visits are about real ale. How many people would visit a giant fizz-factory like Whitbread Magor or Courage Reading? Encouraging brewery visits helps develop the public's appetite for the traditional product.
• A visitors' facility which is profitable in its own right is a valuable addition to any brewery's finances: indeed, tourism potential is written into the mission statements of museum-pieces such as Hoskins of Leicester and Tolly Cobbold of Ipswich.
• Visitors make brewers feel loved – irritated, exasperated, but still loved. The temptation to throw in the towel must be strong when the only voices you hear are gloomy accountants and even gloomier business analysts; maybe appreciative noises from well-satisfied punters might just drown out the pessimists.
• A trip to a brewery makes a fine day out. It might be the architecture that interests you, it may be the engineering, it may be the biosciences, it may just be the beer. But the least visually appealing brewery can reveal the fascinating mysteries of brewing; so even if your nearest brewery is a micro on an industrial estate, lift that phone and book that tour.

Tips On Visiting Breweries

• Book well in advance. Few breweries can cater for individuals turning up unannounced, and most breweries only welcome large pre-booked parties.
• Don't wear anything that matters. Often, brewery tours involve squeezing through tight spaces lined with damp plaster, fresh paint, and the sort of substances which ruin cashmere.
• Wear non-slip shoes. Brewery floors are usually wet.
• Remember that most breweries have had odd vessels and bits of pipework squashed in higgeldy-piggeldy over the years; there are often narrow and steep staircases or even ladders to negotiate. You have to be moderately agile.
• Don't touch anything unless told to.
• Don't breathe in deeply over a fermenter: the CO_2 will sting for hours.

ENGLAND

— Bedfordshire —

B&T BREWERY

THE BREWERY, SHEFFORD, BEDS SG17 5DZ
☎ 01462 815 080
Contact Mike Desquesnes
New brewery on industrial estate.
Tours Summer/Autumn, Mon, Tue, Wed, Thur evenings. Tours last an hour. Max 25. Phone or write to book.

— Buckinghamshire —

REBELLION BEER COMPANY

UNIT J, ROSE INDUSTRIAL ESTATE, MARLOW BOTTOM, MARLOW, BUCKS SL7 3ND
☎ 01628 476 594
Contact Tim Coombes
New brewery on industrial estate.
Tours only available for CAMRA groups and local pubs at £5 per head.
Shop open Mon-Fri 8-6pm, Sat 9-4pm for T-shirts, sweatshirts, pumpclips and beer. Casual visitors welcome.

VALE BREWERY COMPANY

THAME ROAD, HADDENHAM, BUCKS HP23 5ED
☎ 01844 290 008
Contact Phil Stevens
Small purpose-built new brewery.
Group visits (min 20, max 30) arranged on application. £10 per head including free-flow bar and buffet.

ELGOOD & SONS

NORTH BRINK BREWERY, NORTH BRINK, WISBECH, CAMBS PE13 1LN
☎ 01945 583160
Contact Jennifer Elgood
Old-established family brewery in Grade II-listed Georgian former mill on the bank of the River Nene. Many traditional copper brewing vessels still in use. Beautiful gardens. New Visitor Centre with bar opens Spring 1998. Ample free parking.
❥ Admission £4 per head in pre-booked groups, which includes free after-tour sampling.
Shop stocks T-shirts, sweatshirts, ties, glasses, mugs, pins etc.
Open March to October, Mon-Fri 9am-5pm.

OAKHAM ALES

THE BREWERY TAP, 80 WESTGATE, PETERBOROUGH, CAMBS.
☎ 01733 353 300
Contact Jake Douglas
Built in the 1930s, originally a school, then a social security office. Conversion to a large pub with 30-barrel brewery should be complete by October 1997.
❥ The pub will be open all day Mon-Sun. Plenty of parking nearby.
Tours by arrangement.
Badges, T-shirts and carryouts available.
Contact brewery for more information.

— Cheshire —

BURTONWOOD BREWERY

Bold Lane, Burtonwood, Warrington, Cheshire WA5 4PS
☎ 01925 225 131
Contact Rona Woods
Old-established brewery modernised in the late 1980s features a glass-sided brewhouse containing a Briggs three-vessel brewing plant. Now-redundant 1930s brewhouse adjacent leads into 1950s open square fermenting rooms.
Ample parking.
Pre-arranged parties (max 25) on Mon-Thur evenings 7.30-9.30pm (not Dec). Costs £7.50 including buffet and bar (free). Minimum fee £150.

— Cornwall —

ST AUSTELL BREWERY CO

63 Trevarthian Road, St Austell, Cornwall PL25 4BY
☎ 01726 74444
Contact Vicky Crossingham
Victorian tower brewery built in 1893. Ninety-minute tour includes history, video and cooperage demonstration. Extra drinks may be bought at Visitor Centre.
Tours: £4 per head, Easter-Oct, Mon-Fri, 11am and 2pm, by appointment only. Winter tours by arrangement.

— Cumbria —

CONISTON BREWING CO

Coppermines Road, Coniston, Cumbria LA21 8HL
☎ 015394 41133
Contact Ian Bradley
Brewhouse in a converted pigsty beside a river and behind a hotel. Brew plant is a showpiece.
Groups (max 25) should book one week in advance by phone.
No Brewery Tap but nearby pub also selling T-shirts, clocks etc.
Visits all year except Sundays.

JENNINGS BROS

Castle Brewery, Cockermouth CA13 9NE
☎ 01900 821011
Contact Helen Wood or Barbara Sutton
Picturesquely sited brewery built in 1874 and enlarged in 1920s.
Visitors centre open spring, summer, autumn for individuals and groups (pre-booked groups in winter).
Admission £2.90 adults, £1.50 12-18.
Tours 11am and 2pm last about 90 mins and include samples.
Full range of bottled beers and brewery merchandise from shop. No bar.

OLD COTTAGE BEER COMPANY

Unit 3, Hall House Industrial Estate, New Hutton, Kendal, Cumbria LA8 0AN
☎ 01539 724 444
Contact Vic/Helen

New brewery on industrial estate.
🍷 Tours by prior arrangement for groups of up to 30.

YATES BREWERY

GHYLL FARM, WESTNEWTON, CARLISLE, CUMBRIA CA5 3NX
☎ 01697 321 081
Brewery in converted barn in a conservation area.
🍷 Visits by prior arrangement only, max 12.

— Devon —

BRANSCOMBE VALE BREWERY

GREAT SEASIDE FARM, BRANSCOMBE, DEVON EX12 3DP
☎ 01297 680 511
Contact Paul Dimond
Brewery in former cowsheds owned by the National Trust. Only 200 yards from the sea, with clifftop views.
🍷 Tours Nov-Mar, Mon-Fri evenings only. Max 30, min 15. Three weeks' notice required. Fee depends on food and drink required by party.
Brewery Tap at Fountain Head, Branscombe (tel 01297 680 359)

EXE VALLEY BREWERY

SILVERTON, EXETER, DEVON EX5 4HF
☎ 01392 860 406
Contact Guy Sheppard
New brewery in converted farm buildings.
🍷 Visits for pre-arranged groups only, arranged at least one month in advance (evenings, not weekends, not in winter). Min 12 people, max 40. Tour lasts approx 1 hour.
Fee of £2.50 per head includes samples.

MILDMAY BREWERY

HOLBETON, NR PLYMOUTH, DEVON PL8 1NA
☎ 01752 830 302
Contact Steve Millichip
Brewery in converted barns next to Mildmay Colours Inn.
Informal tours for individuals as, when, and if they turn up. Larger parties (up to 20) please phone in advance. Tour approx 45 mins.
No fee for tour with samples. £2.50 if buffet required.
Visits Mon-Fri, afternoon and early evening.

SUMMERSKILLS

15 POMPHLETT FARM INDUSTRIAL ESTATE, BROXTON DRIVE, BILLACOMBE, PLYMOUTH, DEVON PL9 7BG
☎ 01752 481 283
Contact Carl Beeson
New brewery on industrial estate.
Tours for 10-15 people, evenings only on Tues and Wed, April-Sept. Phone to book.
Fee by negotiation.

TEIGNWORTHY BREWERY

TUCKERS MALTINGS, TEIGN ROAD, NEWTON ABBOTT, DEVON TQ12 4AA
☎ 01626 332 066
Contact John Lawton or Brian Gates
New brewery set up to complement historic Tuckers Maltings, a traditional floor-maltings which is open to the public but still fully operational.
Open seven days a week from Good Friday-31 Oct. Guided tours (approx 1 hour) all day, first tour 10.30am, last tour 3pm (3.45pm Bank Hols and July-Sept).
Prices £3.95 adult, £3.65 senior citizen, £2.45 child. Group rates (max 15): £3.55 adult, £3.15 senior citizen, £2.15 child.
Speciality bottled beer shop stocking over 60 British ales

and jams, chutneys, honeys etc containing ale or malt. Mail order facility.
Easy parking.
No need to book in advance (except groups).

— Dorset —

BADGER BREWERY

BOURNEMOUTH ROAD, BLANDFORD ST MARY, DORSET
DT11 9LS
☎ 01258 452 141
Contact Brian Miller
Late Victorian brewery buildings dominate the town. Visitor Centre in Maltings Bar with company memorabilia.
♥ Tours last 2-3 hours, include supper and drinks. Max 30. Book via Brian Miller.
Shop sells full range of alcoholic drinks and limited range of souvenirs.

THOMAS HARDY BREWERY

WEYMOUTH AVENUE, DORCHESTER, DORSET DT1 1QY
☎ 01305 251 251
Contact Mrs S Hutton
Big old-established brewery is a listed building offering a small museum and guided brewery tours.
♥ Tours Mon-Fri at 10.30am, 2.30pm or 7.30pm. Max 35, min 15. (Smaller parties can join other groups.)
Tour lasts approx 75 mins and includes a 20-minute video on the brewing process. Complimentary drink on arrival. Bar in the Maltings open after tour for sampling. Gifts and souvenirs available.
£4 per person. Finger buffet or ploughmans lunch £1.50 extra. Note that brewery floors can be wet and slippery, and suitable footwear should be worn. Also several flights of

stairs to negotiate!
Bookings/further information on 01305 258 207.

PALMERS BREWERY

BRIDPORT, DORSET DT6 4JA
☎ 01308 422 396
Contact Jacky Follett (tel 01308 427 500)
Britain's only thatched brewery; old-established family concern in picturesque town.
♥ £2.50 for tours (max 20), booked in advance by ringing number above or visiting Palmers Wine Store next to brewery.
Tours last two hours and include samples and a certificate.
Four hundred different items stocked in shop.
Visits Apr-Oct, Tue, Wed, Thur mornings.

— Co Durham —

BUTTERKNOWLE BREWERY

THE OLD SCHOOLHOUSE, LYNESACK, BISHOP AUCKLAND DL13 5QF
☎ 01388 710109
Contact Michelle Robinson
New brewery houses in buildings of former Lynesack national School, built 1852, derelict 1962-1989. Brewery opened by John and Sue Constable in 1990. Visitor Centre combines brewing information with displays of memorabilia from local collieries, now all gone.
♥ Pre-booked tours start at 7pm on weekday evenings for parties of up to 30 at £8 a head. Fee includes snacks and samples. Visits last until 9.30pm and are available March-November.

CASTLE EDEN BREWERY

PO Box 13, Castle Eden, Hartlepool, Co Durham TS27 4SX

☎ 01429 839 210

Contact Sylvia or Betty

Whitbread-owned local brewery built in 1826 by John Nimmo in very picturesque rural setting, parts of which have Grade II listing.

Visitor centre with ample parking.

Parties must be pre-booked, min 20, preferably evenings.

Tours last approx two hours.

Fee £6 includes tour and samples.

Good food pub, Castle Eden Inn, in village.

— Essex —

CROUCH VALE BREWERY

12 Redhills Road, South Woodham Ferrers, Chelmsford, Essex CM3 5UP

☎ 01245 322 744

Contact Colin Bocking or Olly Graham

New brewery on industrial estate.

Parties of 15, Mon-Thur evenings 7pm (or earlier), 90 mins duration. No tours during winter months. Trade or CAMRA groups only.

No fee for tour. Buffet can be arranged at local pub.

RIDLEY'S

Hartford End brewery, Hartford End, Chelmsford CM3 1TZ

☎ 01371 820316

Contact: Paula Partridge

Attractive 154-year-old country tower brewery with many

old copper vessels. Clock House Visitor Centre with bar and shop in former dray sheds.

🍺 Pre-booked tours in organised groups of 12-20 only, available Mon-Fri. Daytime tours 11am and 2.30pm at £3 a head, evening tours £5 a head, 6.30pm.

— Gloucestershire —

FREEMINER BREWERY

THE LAURELS, SLING, COLEFORD, ROYAL FOREST OF DEAN

☎ 01594 810 408

Contact Don Burgess

🍺 Tours of 25-30 people (min 10) booked with eight weeks' notice. Duration dependent on academic level. Fee negotiable according to requirements (eg buffet, barbecue). Brewery Tap (5 mins walk) sells food, bottled beer, souvenirs. The Wine Barrel at Coleford sells bottled beers, T-shirts etc.

Visits usually weekday evenings, weekends by special prior arrangement.

— Hampshire —

CHERITON BREWHOUSE

BRANDY MOUNT, CHERITON, ALRESFORD, HAMPSHIRE
SO24 0QQ

☎ 01962 771 166

Contact Martin Roberts

Purpose-built barn in farmyard setting at the Flowerpots Inn, Cheriton, an early 19th century farmhouse.

🍺 No fee for visits but please book in advance through brewery.

GEORGE GALE & CO

THE HAMPSHIRE BREWERY, HORNDEAN, HANTS PO8 0DA
☎ 01705 571 212
Contact Jenny Charman
Traditional 150 year old Victorian working brewery. Open wooden fermenting vessels, traditional mash tun and copper, and 19th-century steam engine once used to power the brewery. Fine collection of old photographs and brewery items on display. Old hop store used as Visitor Centre.
Visitors should book in advance but walk-in tours offered on Tuesday mornings May-Sept for small groups only. Charge £3.50 per person includes tour of approx two hours and sampling of beer and country wines. Discount for groups of 20-50.
Brewery shop sells HSB, Prize Old Ale, T-shirts, sweatshirts, tankards, jugs and other memorabilia plus Old Country Wines. Ship and Bell Hotel next door is open all day.
Tours all year, Mon-Fri and Sat mornings at 10.30 and 2.30.
Free parking.

HAMPSHIRE BREWERY LTD

6/8 ROMSEY INDUSTRIAL ESTATE, GREATBRIDGE ROAD, ROMSEY, HANTS
☎ 01794 83000
Contact Jeff Schofield
New brewery on industrial estate.
Tours twice weekly throughout the year, Tue and Thur 6.30-8pm. Recommended group size 20-30. Book in advance.
Fee £3.50 including sampling.
Shop sells all cask beer products plus small but interesting range of bottles.

RINGWOOD BREWERY

138 Christchurch Road, Ringwood, Hants BH24 3AP
☎ 01425 471 177
Contact Lisa Winkworth
Located in attractive 18th-century buildings, originally Tunk's Brewery, in market town on the edge of the New Forest.
♥ Tours for 20 min, 40 people max. Tour lasts approx 45 minutes plus sampling after.
Fee £5.25 for tour, sampling and ploughmans.
Shop open 9.30-5pm, selling clothing, breweriana and Ringwood beers plus selection of other beers and country wines. Also has Pin Room bar for tasting.
Tours Tue evenings 6.30pm (not July and August). Waiting list currently rather long.

SPIKES BREWERY

43-47 Albert Road, Southsea, Portsmouth, Hants PO5 2SF
☎ 01705 864 712
Contact Jim Wimpress
Brewery above Wine Vaults pub with 12 revolving real ales.
Prebooked tours for 20 max, Mon-Sun 9am-8pm.

— Hertfordshire —

MCMULLEN & SONS

26 Old Cross, Hertford, Herts SG14 1RD
☎ 01992 584 911
Contact Dennis Ruttledge
Traditional red brick Victorian tower brewery built in 1891.
♥ Pre-booked visits for parties of 14. Preference given to groups from within the company trading area. A museum is

part of the hospitality suite.
No fee.
Brewery shop sells brewery memorabilia and the bar is free.
Visits throughout the year on Mondays from 10am-2.30pm including lunch.

— Kent —

FLAGSHIP BREWERY

UNIT 2, BUILDING 64, THE HISTORIC DOCKYARD, CHATHAM, KENT ME4 4TE
☎ 01634 832 828
Contact Andrew Purcell
The brewery, although not of particular architectural interest itself, is sited within the Historic Dockyard which is a preserved Georgian dockyard open to visitors. Brewery display area showing brewing process is open to all visitors to the Dockyard.
Formal tours and talks for groups (max 40) weekday evenings or Saturdays year-round – book in advance.
T-shirts, sweatshirts, keyrings, pumpclips sold at brewery.
No bar or brewery tap but beer available at Wheelwrights Restaurant in Dockyard.

P&DJ GOACHER

UNIT 8, TOVIL GREEN BUSINESS PARK, MAIDSTONE, KENT ME15 6DT
☎ 01622 682 112
Contact Phil Goacher
New brewery on industrial estate.
Brewery visits by appointment, generally on weekday evenings only. Preference given to local groups. Tour and talk last about an hour.
No shop or brewery tap, but there is a pub nearby.

LARKINS BREWERY

CHIDDINGSTONE, EDENBRIDGE, KENT TN8 7BB
☎ 01892 870 328
Contact Bob Dockerty
Converted farm buildings, part of the Lord Astor of Hever's estate. The village of Chiddingstone is very old and is owned by the National Trust.
♥ Organised parties (max 15) on Saturday mornings, 10.30-12, by appointment (not Aug or Sep). Tasting of all beers.
Fee £5 per person
Meals available at local pubs.
Good parking.

SHEPHERD NEAME

17 COURT STREET, FAVERSHAM, KENT ME13 7AX
☎ 01795 532 206
Contact Mr J Gray
Britain's oldest brewery – brewing on site since 1698.
Reception Centre has medieval origins.
♥ Tours by appointment only, approx 45 minutes plus sampling.
Parties of 32 max (daytime), 40 (evening).
Fee £2 includes sampling plus cheese and biscuits and/or crisps.
T-shirts, tankards, jugs, keyrings etc plus bottled and canned products.
Times: Mon-Thur 10.30am, 2.30pm, 7.30pm; Fri 10.30am only.
Town car and coach parks nearby.

— Lancashire —

HART BREWERY

Cartford Hotel, Cartford Lane, Little Eccleston, Lancs
☎ 01995 671 686
Contact John Smith
Brewery in hotel outbuildings.
❢ Tours for groups of 10-50, booked in advance, starting 6.30pm Mon-Thur evenings. Duration two hours.
£3.50 per person including souvenir glass and two pints of beer.
No shop but T-shirts available in Brewery Tap.

MOORHOUSES BREWERY

4 Moorhouse Street, Burnley, Lancashire BB11 5EN
☎ 01282 422 864
Contact Mr R Lee
Modern brewing plant incorporating two old coppers dating back to 1919.
❢ Parties of 15-30 people by prior appointment. Booking forms sent on request.
Fee £4 per person including tour, three pints of different Moorhouses beers and pie and peas supper.
Leisure wear often available for purchase.
Further drinks can be purchased at the bar.
Visits all year (except 20 December-3 January) on Tue, Wed or Thur evenings at 7.30pm. Other times can be organised by special arrangement only.

ROSSENDALE BREWERY

Griffin Inn, 84 Hud Rake, Haslingden, Lancashire
☎ 01706 214 021

Contact David Porter

♦ Tours for 12 max. Last one hour. No fee. Pub attached. Tours any time but Fri evenings.

— Leicestershire & Rutland —

EVERARDS BREWERY

CASTLE ACRES, NARBOROUGH, LEICESTER LE9 5BY
☎ 0116 201 4100
Contact Helen Pickwell
Old-established family firm in brand-new premises on by-pass.

♦ Brewery visits restricted to organised parties from pubs stocking Everards ales and from branches of CAMRA. Advanced booking necessary. Weekday visits only, preferably Tue, Wed or Thur 10.30am-2.30pm. £6.50 per head includes lunch and free ale. Min 12, max 24. Free parking.

THE GRAINSTORE BREWERY

DAVIS'ES BREWING CO LTD, STATION APPROACH, OAKHAM, RUTLAND
☎ 01572 770 065
Contact Mr Sharkey
Restored grainstore with original cast iron columns and wooden floors. Three-storey building has two floors and a cellar for brewing and racking, with a Brewery Tap on the ground floor.

♦ Groups up to 50 catered for, with a range of buffet and tasting menus. Tours normally 30 minutes to an hour depending upon technical interest.
Fee dependent on type of tour selected.
Tours at any time by prior arrangement and subject to availability.

TOM HOSKINS BREWERY

133 Beaumanor Road, Leicester LE4 5QE
☎ 0116 266 1122
Contact Mr A Allen
Traditional neighbourhood brewery is operated as a working museum and visitors are welcome to see the brewing process as it was a century ago. Many items from the past are on display, including 18th and 19th century coopers' tools from France and England and cask branding irons.
Evening tours (Mon-Fri) starting 7.15pm for groups (min age 18) of eight to 30. Tour includes slide presentation narrated by Raymond Baxter and meal accompanied by a pint of Hoskins bitter.
Quality home-cooked food and fine beers available in two splendid bars, the Tom Hoskins Tap Room and the Grist Room, with its plush, comfortable seating and friendly atmosphere.
Advance booking essential.
Fees payable in advance (phone to check prices).

PARISH BREWERY

Old Brewery Inn, Somerby, nr Melton Mowbray, Leics LE14 2PZ
☎ 01664 454 781
Contact Baz Parish
Brewery in courtyard of old posting inn.
Fee £1.50 for tour only (minimum 12) or tour and buffet (minimum 12) at £6.
Baz's Brewers Dozen: evening tour of brewery plus large buffet of Leicestershire's finest fare, beer included. Min 12, max 75. Cost £18 each. For every 12 people booked, one extra person is free.
Free wine or soft drinks for non-beer drinkers.
Book in advance. 10% deposit required, payable to Mainline Leisure Ltd, remainder payable by cash or credit card on

arrival for visit. Final numbers must be confirmed at least 3-4 days prior to visit.
Full parking facilities. Coaches welcome.

RUDDLES BREWERY

LANGHAM, OAKHAM, RUTLAND, LEICS **LE15 7JD**
☎ 01572 756 911
Contact Barbara Reynolds
Brewery first established in 1858; many original buildings still intact and in use. Brewery in tiny village of Langham, surrounded by picturesque countryside. Original family home still used today as company headquarters.
♥ Visitor centre, recently refurbished, includes a reception area and a bar located in the original cellars, retaining the brewery's historic feel.
Tours £10 including brewhouse visit, lunch or supper and drinks. Groups of 12-40. CAMRA discount price £7.50.
Ample free parking.
Brewery merchandise from T-shirts to jackets and take-home beer available, all at favourable prices.
Tours all year round, Tue, Wed, Thur, afternoon or evening.
Other times by arrangement.
Book in advance.

— Lincolnshire —

GEORGE BATEMAN & SON

SALEM BRIDGE BREWERY, MILL LANE, WAINFLEET, SKEGNESS, LINCS **PE24 4JE**
☎ 01754 880 317
Contact Sandra Raymond
Brewery is based on an old windmill and a Georgian coach-house. Picturesquely sited beside Tennyson's Brook.
Includes small museum.

Pre-booked tour groups of 12-36 welcome 7pm Mon-Thur; £10 a head includes samples and pie, chips and peas supper. Also available at £30 a head, weekend visit including night's B&B.
Shop selling bottled beers and branded merchandise; no bar.

— Greater London —

FULLER SMITH & TURNER

GRIFFIN BREWERY, CHISWICK, LONDON W4 2QB
☎ 0181 996 2063
Contact Susan Neville Jones
Griffin Brewery in Chiswick claims to be London's oldest brewery (but then so does Young's). History has it that a brewery has stood on the site since the time of Oliver Cromwell. It has been controlled by the Fullers, Smiths and Turners for over 150 years, with direct descendants of the founding families still involved in running the company today. It is also a brewery where the writer Alexander Pope had a summer house, the remains of which are still visible. Dick Turpin regularly passed on his route to wreak havoc on carriages heading west. The oldest wisteria in the country clings lovingly to the brickwork.
❦ Tours begin in the Mawson Arms on the corner of the brewery. There you will be met by your guide and taken on a comprehensive tour explaining the brewing process. After the tour, visitors are taken to the Hock Cellar, where many interesting artefacts and memorabilia are on view. It is there too that you can sample Fuller's range of draught real ales. Advance booking essential for all groups and strongly recommended for individuals. (Tours not suitable for those with impaired mobility.)
No parking at Mawson Arms but roadside parking available on both sides of the A4. Note that the River Thames can flood Chiswick Mall at high tide, so check tide

details if parking there. Nearest Underground is Turnham Green (District Line), a 15 minute walk. Alternatively Stamford Brook (also District Line) and take 190 bus. Chiswick Station is closest main line train. E3, H91, 27, 237, 267, 391 go to Chiswick High Road. 190 bus from Hammersmith stops almost outside brewery.

Tours last approx 90 minutes. £5 per head, £67.50 per group of 15. Free to members of CAMRA. Tickets include a £1 voucher redeemable either in the Mawson Arms towards the price of a Fuller's London Pride, or £1 off purchases over £5 on Fuller's merchandise at the brewery store. Tour ends in brewery store which carries extensive range of brewing souvenirs, clothing, wines and beers. Groups can then return to the Mawson Arms for a drink and a meal. Tours on Mon, Wed, Thur, Fri starting promptly at 10am, 11am, 1pm and 2pm.

SCANLON'S BREWERY

Unit 8D, Rainbow Industrial Estate, Trout Road, Yiewsley, Middlesex UB7 7XT

☎ 01895 256 270

Contact Jerry Scanlon

Brewery overlooks Grand Union canal and has lots of pleasure boats passing during the warmer months.

Visitors always welcome free of charge. Prior notice for larger groups appreciated.

Ample parking after 5pm and at weekends.

Maximum tour size 20. Duration 30 minutes approx.

YOUNG & CO

Ram Brewery, Wandsworth High Street, Wandsworth, London SW18 4JD

☎ 0181 875 7005

Contact John Wheater

Beer brewed on site for over 400 years. Two Victorian coppers, two magnificent 19th-century working steam-

driven beam engines. Young's also has London's last remaining cooperage where wooden barrels used to be made and are still repaired. Much of the beer is delivered locally by horse-drawn dray. Twenty working dray horses, mainly Shires, share the brewery stables with a ram, goats, a pony and a donkey. A farrier makes all the horses' shoes in the smithy behind the stables.
The Brewery Tap, Young's Visitor Centre, is open seven days a week. Full range of Young's products, leisure wear, ties, glasses, horseshoes, books and more plus draught and bottled beer and fine wines. Meals available.
Tours 10am, 12noon, 2pm, 4pm, seven days a week.
Full brewery tours (lasting approx 75 minutes): £5.50 adults; £4.50 pensioners and students; £3.50 14-17 year olds (who must be accompanied by an adult). Price includes beer samples and half-pint of beer or a soft drink.
Family tour of stables (approx 45 minutes): £3.50 adults; £2 children under 18 (must be accompanied by an adult); Family ticket £9; children under 5 no charge. Payment by Visa, Mastercard, American Express, Switch or cash.
Tailor-made packages available for organised groups, company meetings or for entertaining. Phone for details.
Please note brewery tour is unsuitable for those with impaired mobility.
Parking at NCP opposite.

— Greater Manchester —

BANK TOP BREWERY

Unit 1, Back Lane, off Vernon Street, Bolton, BL1 2LD
☎ 01204 528 865
Contact John Feeney
New brewery on industrial estate.
❦ Tours meet at Howcroft Inn, Pool Street at 7.30pm. Parties 10-30 people. Tour lasts two hours, with drinks. £5 per head,

drinks in brewery, supper at Howcroft Inn which has full size bowling green. Visits Mon-Fri, all year round. Howcroft 7.30pm, Brewery 8pm, Howcroft 10pm.

HYDES ANVIL BREWERY

46 Moss Lane West, Manchester M15 5PH
☎ 0161 226 1317
Contact Charles Cook
Typical English tower brewery built between 1860 and 1870.
Tours for pre-booked parties of 15-25 last up to 90 minutes. Usually only one party per week, and booked up well in advance.
No fee but bar for the enjoyment of !

JW LEES & CO

Greengate Brewery, Middleton Junction, Manchester M24 2AX
☎ 0161 643 2487
Contact Giles Dennis
Traditional Victorian brewery, one of the most modern in the country when built in 1876. Still very traditional.
Weekly brewery tours, by arrangement only.

FREDERIC ROBINSON

Unicorn Brewery, Stockport SK1 1JJ
☎ 0161 480 6571
Contact Lee Carr
Prominent town centre brewery, older parts of offices dating back over 100 years.
Brewery tours in evenings. Party max 25. Tours booked in writing to brewery, when available dates will be given.
Fee of £2.50 includes small introduction, tour of brewery, small sample of Robinsons beers.
Unicorn Wine Shop adjoining offices. Collectors items such as T-shirts always available.
Tours all year round except for busy times and holidays.

— Merseyside —

ROBERT CAIN BREWERY

STANHOPE STREET, LIVERPOOL L8 5XJ
☎ 0151 709 8734
Contact Mrs J Shaw
Grade II listed tower brewery with CAMRA design award-winning Brewery Tap.
♥ Tours Mon-Thur evenings at 6.30pm all year round. Fee of £3.95 includes buffet and two pints. Contact Mrs J Shaw for bookings.

— Norfolk —

BUFFY'S BREWERY

MARDLE HALL, RECTORY ROAD, TIVETSHALL ST MARY, NORFOLK NR15 2DD
☎ 01379 676 523
Contact Julie Savory
Small brewery in outbuilding next to 15th century timber-framed house.
♥ Parties, max 20, welcome by prior arrangement. £5 fee includes all beer (tea or coffee for drivers). T-shirts and polypins of beer available.

CHALK HILL BREWERY

ROSARY ROAD, NORWICH NR1 4DA
☎ 01603 477 078
Traditional exterior to brewery which is attached to the Coach & Horses dating back to 1814 and Grade II listed.
♥ Minimum two weeks' notice for tours. Max 20. Tour lasts 20-40 minutes plus complimentary tasting, then buy and drink as required at paying bar.

ICENI BREWERY

3 Foulden Road, Ickburgh, nr Mundford, Norfolk IP26 5BJ

☎ 01842 878 922

Contact Brendan Moore

Brewery situated at edge of Thetford Forest.

Parties up to 30 people. Tour lasts an hour. Book in advance.

Fee £2.50 including sample of ales.

T-shirts and some printed material on sale.

Tours Mon, Fri, Sat all year round from 2pm, evenings included.

REEPHAM BREWERY

Unit 1, Collers Way, Reepham, Norwich, Norfolk

☎ 01609 871 091

Contact Ted Willems

New brewery on industrial estate.

Groups (max 20) by prior arrangement. Tour lasts an hour.

No shop.

THE WOLF BREWERY

10 Maurice Gaymer Road, Attleborough, Norfolk NR17 2QZ

☎ 01953 457 775

Contact Wolfe J Witham

Brewery on site of old Gaymer's Cider orchard (Gaymer's factory closed 1996 after 700 years).

Parties of up to 15 usually on weekday evenings (preferably Tue and Wed). Tour lasts approx 90 minutes with tastings. Write or phone for details.

Excellent CAMRA guide hotel (five minutes from brewery) provides sandwiches and good range of ales to finish tour.

No fee for tour but sandwiches at hotel are extra.

WOODFORDE'S NORFOLK ALES

BROADLAND BREWERY, WOODBASTWICK, NORWICH NR13 6SW
☎ 01603 720 353
Contact Sandra Bruce-Smith (tours); Howard Miller (shop)
Brewery is based around a group of traditional farm buildings in Woodbastwick village and has its own borehole.
Visitor centre stocks take-home containers and bottled beers, brewery memorabilia, clothing, posters and a wide range of locally-produced preserves etc. No admission charge. Open 10.30am-4pm.
Brewery Tap at adjacent Fur & Feather Inn has reputation for excellent and plentiful food.
Brewery tours on Tue and Thur evenings start at 7pm, lasting approx 90 minutes. Guide will give in-depth history of Woodforde's and cover all aspects of brewing and the brewery, welcoming any questions. Sampling after in the Visitor centre, then to Fur & Feather Inn for a free pint.
Corporate booking system for groups of 10-12 (regular), or up to 20-24 (large group).
Fee £45 regular group; £90 large group. £10 deposit on booking, balance payable no later than 14 days prior to visit, with confirmation of numbers attending.
Tours all year, Tue/Thur at 7pm.

— Northumberland —

BORDER BREWERY CO

THE OLD KILN, BREWERY LANE, TWEEDMOUTH, BERWICK ON TWEED, TD15 2AH
☎ 01289 303 303
Contact Andy Burrows/Mark Satchwell

Brewery is on site of former brewery maltings dating back to 1777.
Tour lasts 20-30 minutes, followed by drinks in Hospitality Bar. Fee of £6 includes four pints, choice of two beers; £8 includes four pints plus pie and pea supper.
Groups (10-20) welcome all year round, preferably evenings. Must book well in advance.

— Nottinghamshire —

HARDYS & HANSONS PLC

KIMBERLEY BREWERY, NOTTINGHAM NG16 2NS
☎ 0115 938 3611
Contact Tony Bourke or George Tunney
The existing Kimberley brewery was built in 1861 and is a fine example of a traditional cask ale brewery.
❢ Groups of 20 for guided tours, followed, where applicable, by sampling beer. Priority to trade/CAMRA visits, educational trips, public service groups (police, ambulance etc) then to other bona fide groups.
No fee.
Tours generally one evening per week, starting at 6.30pm, although can be flexible.

MALLARD BREWERY

15 HARTINGTON AVENUE, CARLTON, NOTTINGHAM NG4 3NR
☎ 0115 952 289
Contact Phil or Gill Mallard
Tiny new brewery.
❢ Small parties up to 10 people throughout the year by appointment.
No fee at present.
T-shirts, pumpclips and posters available.

MANSFIELD BREWERY

Littleworth, Mansfield, Notts NG18 1AB
☎ 01623 25691
Visitor centre currently under development and scheduled to open in 1998.
❣ Public visits on the second Sunday of each month. Tour of 45 minutes followed by brief sampling session. Max 30 people.
No fee at present.
Must book well in advance.

MAYPOLE BREWERY

North Laithes Farm, Wellow Road, Eakring, Newark, Notts NG22 0AW
☎ 01623 871 690
Contact Danny Losinski
Brewery in converted farm building.
❣ Visits by arrangement (max 20) on Friday evenings and Sunday lunchtimes.
£3.50 per person including brief talk on brewing and drinks. Usually end in local pub stocking range of Maypole beers.

— Oxfordshire —

WH BRAKSPEAR & SONS

The Brewery, New Street, Henley-on-Thames, Oxon RG9 2BU
☎ 01491 573 636
Contact Mrs Evaline King
Victorian brewery in centre of historic Thames Valley town. Wine cellars in brewery yard are open to the public. Well stocked off-licence also selling Brakspear memorabilia. No on-site bar, but 16 Brakspear houses within 10 minutes' walk. Brewery tours may be introduced early 1998.

CHILTERN VALLEY

OLD LUXTERS VINEYARD, WINERY & BREWERY, HAMBLEDEN, HENLEY-ON-THAMES, OXON RG9 6JW
☎ 01491 638 330
Contact David Ealand
New winery and brewery incorporating barn, c1700, now fine-art gallery.
♥ Complete and practical explanation of wine production techniques from grape to glass, lasting 1-2 hours. Includes walk around vineyard, winery, brewing and bottling facilities. Taste award-winning wines (and real ale by request) in gallery.
£7 per person include VAT. Reservation confirmed on £25 deposit.
Guided tours of vineyard, winery and brewery (minimum 15 people), on weekday evenings from 6pm and at weekends, by prior arrangement. Summer and winter times may vary.
Traditional meals can be booked at local pubs serving Chiltern Valley beers: the Frog at Skirmett, 01491 638996, and Stag & Huntsman, 01491 571227. Alternatively, meals can be arranged at the brewery.
Shop open 9-5.30 weekdays, 11-5.30 weekends.
Parking for cars or minibuses and a coach.

HOOK NORTON BREWERY CO

THE BREWERY, HOOK NORTON, BANBURY, OXON OX15 5NY
☎ 01608 737 120
Contact Paula Clarke
Highly traditional late Victorian tower brewery with much original equipment including steam engine; on edge of pretty Cotswold village.
♥ Tours (max 12) promptly at 10am or 7.30pm, booked in advance.
Fee £2.50 per person.

Shop sells all point-of-sale and promotional goods.
Accommodation and food available at brewery's pubs in Hook Norton village: Sun Inn, tel 01608 737 570 and Pear Tree, 01608 737 482. Food also available at the Gate Hangs High, 01608 737 387 on the outskirts of the village. Pubs also have Aunt Sally and/or skittles.

MORRELLS BREWERY

St Thomas Street, Oxford OX1 1LA
☎ 01865 813 036
Contact Christopher Whitehouse
Parts of the brewery date back to the 16th century. There has been a brewery on the site since 1452. The Morrell family has been brewing on the site since 1743. Impressive brewery gates plus a 19th century boiling copper in daily use.
Tours begin in the Brewery Gate pub. From there you are taken next door to the brewery itself where old and new technology are combined. Expert guides unlock the secrets of the brewer's art as you taste the malt, and smell the hops and yeast. You may meet Morrells' very own 'Fat Cat' – the brewery's mouser! After the tour, you can sample the final product in the traditional atmosphere of the Brewery Gate, where you can stay to enjoy a drink and a traditional pub meal. In winter there is a real log fire and in the summer you can enjoy the view of Oxford Castle and the Mill Stream from the beer garden.
The Brewery Shop sells an extensive range of brewing souvenirs, clothes, books and a wide variety of pub wares.
Brewery Gate open 8am-11pm Mon-Fri; 11am-3pm and 7-11pm Sat; 12-3pm Sun.
Walk-in tours: 1 July-31 August, Tue-Sat at 12pm and 2pm (no 2pm tour on Sat). 1 September-30 June, Sats only at 12pm. No tours over Christmas/New Year period.
Tours last approx one hour. Tickets available from Brewery Gate pub.
Group Bookings: tours for groups of more than 10 can be arranged at other times. Advanced booking for groups

essential. Buffet meals can be arranged for groups of more than 15. Call 01865 813 036 to book. No group tours on Sun or Mon. No tours over Christmas/New Year period.
Fee £3.75 adults, £2.75 for 14-17 year olds (no under 14s admitted).
Group adult £3.50, group 14-17 year olds £2.50.
Adult price includes samples and free half pint of beer or soft drink in Brewery Gate.

— Shropshire —

WOOD BREWERY

PLOUGH INN, WISTANSTOW, CRAVEN ARMS, SHROPSHIRE SY7 8DG
☎ 01588 672 523
Contact Edward Wood
Brewery in brick-built former stock shed adjoining pub.
♥ Organised groups by arrangement, usually mid-week evenings.
Fee variable but includes sampling
Various items for sale at Plough Inn.

HOBSONS BREWERY

NEWHOUSE FARM, TENBURY ROAD, CLEOBURY MORTIMER, SALOP
☎ 01299 270 837
Contact Nick Davis
Converted former granary, heavily beamed.
♥ Groups up to 24, approx 90 minutes, evenings only. Book in advance.
Limited selection of shorts, jugs etc available. No paying bar.

— Somerset —

ASH VINE BREWERY

THE WHITE HART, TRUDOXHILL, FROME, SOMERSET BA11 5DP
☎ 01373 836 744
Contact Robert Viney
Brewery at back of 17th century White Hart Inn.
Free tours available for visitors eating at the pub. Prior booking required, giving one month's notice. Individuals and groups welcome. Most Ash Vine beers on sale in White Hart. Tours Mon-Thur (lunchtime and evening); Fri (lunchtimes).

COTLEIGH BREWERY

FORD ROAD, WIVELISCOMBE, SOMERSET TA4 2RE
☎ 01984 624 086
Contact Roly Willett
Pre-arranged visits (max 25) only from pubs with which brewery is currently trading.
No fee but donation to nominated charity, currently the Hawk and Owl Trust.

MOOR BEER COMPANY

WHITLEY FARM, ASHCOTT, BRIDGWATER, SOMERSET
☎ 01458 40050
Contact Annette
Brewery in converted woodworking shop on farm.
Please phone to arrange visits.

RCH BREWERY

WEST HEWISH, NR WESTON SUPER MARE, SOMERSET BS24 6RR
☎ 01934 834 447

Contact Paul Davey
❦ Brewery tours for groups of 20-25 on Tue and Thur evenings only.

THE BASS MUSEUM

HORNINGLOW STREET, BURTON UPON TRENT, STAFFS DE14 7QD
☎ 01283 511 000
Contact Sharon Stokes
The Bass Museum has several exhibitions showing the story of brewing and transportation. Features include model of Burton-upon-Trent 1921, a reconstructed Edwardian bar, The Brewing Gallery, historic fleet of horse-drawn and motorised vehicles. Oldest working micro brewery in Britain, with equipment dating back to 1830, 1905 Robey steam engine and the Joiners Shop with many hands-on and visual displays. Home of famous Bass shire horses. Well-stocked souvenir shop, restaurant and licensed bars.
❦ Open 10am-5pm every day except Christmas, Boxing Day, New Year's Day.
Admission to Visitor Centre and Museum, adult £3.75, senior citizen £2.50, child £2, family ticket (two adults and up to three children) £9.95. Group rate (parties of 15): adult £3.25. senior citizen £2, child £1.50. Admission includes free glass of beer, lager, soft drink, tea or coffee.
Admission to Visitor Centre, Museum and Brewery Tour, adult £5.50, senior citizen £4.25, child (over 15) £3.75. Admission includes free glass of beer, lager, soft drink, coffee or tea. Admission to Museum, Visitor Centre and Brewery Tour with sampling session, adult £6.75, senior citizen £6.75, child (over 15) £6.75. Admission includes 3 pints of beer, lager or soft drinks.
Brewery Tours should be booked in advance.
Ample parking for cars and coaches.

CARLSBERG-TETLEY BURTON BREWERY

107 Station Street, Burton upon Trent, Staffs DE14 1BZ
☎ 01283 502 500
Contact Mrs Ruby Heeps
Brewing on this site since 1856. Samuel Allsopps brewery is in middle of brewery (now C-T Burton Brewery, formerly Ind Coope Burton brewery). Tour takes in whole process from brewing to packaging.
Visitor Centre was the original Samuel Allsopps cellars which have been beautifully refurbished. Caters mainly for organised groups of 20-80. Tour and drink £5.50; tour and meal £9, reductions for children (school parties, not under 13 years).
T-shirts, pens, keyrings, bags, lighters etc available at shop.
Paying bar on site.
Visits Mon-Fri except Christmas and Bank Holidays.

MARSTON THOMPSON & EVERSHED

The Brewery, Shobnall Road, Burton-on-Trent, Staffs DE14 2BW
☎ 01283 531 131
Visitor centre due for official opening late 1997. Once open brewery visits will be marketed to the public, offering group tours and a mini-conference centre.

TITANIC BREWERY

Harvey Works, Lingard Street, Burslem, Staffs ST6 1ED
☎ 01782 823 447
Contact Ian Bradford
New brewery in part of old engineering works.
Organised evening/weekend tours (25 max) available, booked in advance.
Fee: Mon-Thur evening £15 per group; Fri-Sun evening £20 per group.
Tour lasts approx 75 minutes and covers brewery history

and development. Beer for consumption during the tour is sold by the cask, ie two, 4.5, nine or 18 gallons, and must be ordered in advance.
Buffet after the tour at Bulls Head, Burslem, where the complete range of Titanic ales may be sampled. Buffet price £3 per head and must be booked and confirmed before tour.

— Suffolk —

GREEN JACK BREWING CO

Unit 2, Harbour Road Industrial Estate, Oulton Broad, Lowestoft, Suffolk NR32 3LZ
☎ 01502 587 905
Contact Tim Dunford
New brewery on industrial estate.
❦ Tours by prior arrangement.
No shop, but Tap Room, live bands, DJs at weekends.
Times: Mon-Fri 5-11pm, summer; 7-11pm, winter;
Sat 1-11pm, summer; 5-11pm winter; Sun 7pm-10.30pm.

ST PETERS BREWERY

St Peters Hall, St Peter South Elmham, Bungay, Suffolk NR35 1NQ
☎ 01986 782 322
Contact Richard Eyton-Jones
Brewery in renovated Grade II listed agricultural buildings, with medieval thatched bar, built around a brick courtyard. Layout gives the visitor a clear understanding of how beer is brewed.
❦ Visitor Centre planned for 1998 but visitors welcome to look round brewery as private parties or at weekends when the 16th-century hall is open to the public.
Parties of 20+ may book midweek tours. Duration approx 1-2 hours including tour of St Peters Hall.

£5 per head for tour and sampling. Food provided at extra cost depending on requirements.
Brewery souvenirs available.
Hall has full on-licence.
Ample parking.

TOLLY COBBOLD

CLIFF QUAY BREWERY, CLIFF ROAD, IPSWICH, SUFFOLK IP3 0AZ
☎ 01473 231 723
Contact the Brewery Guides
Magnificent Victorian tower brewery on the banks of the River Orwell, in the middle of the city's docklands regeneration area. The brewery was briefly closed and reopened partly as a museum, with Tap and visitors centre in 18th-century Brewer's House adjoining.
Tours for casual visitors start at noon May-Sept at £3.75 per head including sample; times of casual tours vary 1 Oct-30 April – ring ahead.
Pre-booked organised tours for parties; discounts for groups of 10 or more. Group tours run year-round 10am-8pm.
Minimum age 14.
Shop carries a wide range of brewery items and local produce. paying bars in popular Brewery Tap.
Ample parking.

— Surrey —

HOGS BACK BREWERY

MANOR FARM, THE STREET, TONGHAM, SURREY GU10 1DE
☎ 01252 783 000
Contact Mary White
Restored Surrey brick and flint barns, circa 1768. Originally large farmhouse and outhouses before conversion to brewery. Haunted by local landlady! All brewing vessels

wooden cladded, in sympathy with age of building.
♥ Visitor Centre/Viewing Gallery to meet and to view brewing process prior to brewery tour. Tours last 90 minutes and cost £4.75 per person. Ample parking for 100 cars and six 54-seater coaches. All tours must be booked in advance. Groups up to 25 per tour, but individuals can also book. Tours fully conducted. Generous beer sampling of 5-7 different real ales with light snacks between to clear palate. Large Brewery Shop with own draught beers and merchandise plus a huge range of Belgian and other bottled beers from around the world. Take-away off licence facility. No paying bar.
Tours Wed and Fri evenings 6.30pm; Sat 11am and 2.30pm; Sun 2.30pm throughout the year. Other times and dates by arrangement.

— Sussex —

ARUNDEL BREWERY

Unit C7, Ford Airfield Estate, Ford, Arundel, West Sussex BN18 0BE
☎ 01903 733 111
Contact Peter Bond
♥ Brewery tours Mon-Wed, commence 6.30-7.30pm. Min 12, max 25. £7.50 per head includes samples and supper at Brewery Tap at Swan Hotel, High Street, Arundel.

BALLARDS BREWERY

The Old Sawmill, Nyewood, Petersfield, Hampshire GU31 5HA
☎ 01730 821 301
Contact Carola Brown
New brewery on industrial estate. Postally Hampshire, actually West Sussex.

♥ Visitors welcome at brewery for off sales, weekdays 8.30-4pm and weekends by arrangement (draught beer should be ordered in advance).
Tours for parties of 12-30, weekday evenings, approx 7.30-9.30. Book in advance.
£4.50 per head for tour plus samples. Shop sells T-shirts, sweatshirts, tankards, keyrings etc.

CUCKMERE HAVEN BREWERY

Golden Galleon, Exceat Bridge, Cuckmere Haven, East Sussex BN25 4AB
☎ 01323 892 247
Contact Alan Edgar
Tiny brewery in pub outbuilding.
♥ Parties welcome, preferably in spring or summer.
Brewery tour limited to six due to size of plant. No fee.
Groups typically go for snack and beer in GBG-listed Golden Galleon next door. Please book in advance.

HARVEY & SON

The Bridge Wharf Brewery, 6 Cliffe High Street, Lewes, East Sussex BN7 2AH
☎ 01273 480 209
Contact Susan Glen-Bott
Set on the River Ouse in the medieval Cliffe area of Lewes, Harveys is a beautiful example of a Victorian country brewery in the Gothic style.
♥ Two groups of 25 people are combined for each tour.
Tours last 90 minutes, followed by informal sampling. By appointment only; no fee.
Brewery Shop open Mon-Sat 9.30am-4.30pm only. Full range of beers, souvenirs etc. Information provided on nearby tied houses serving food.
Tours April-Nov, weekday evenings Mon-Wed starting 6.30 and ending 8.45.

KING & BARNES

18 BISHOPRIC, HORSHAM, WEST SUSSEX RH12 1QP
☎ 01403 270 470
Contact Sally Richardson
150 year old town centre brewery, heavily modernised.
♦ Tours Mon-Fri for organised groups (max 30) last 90 minutes. Booking deposit required.
£3 day tour, £5 evenings (both include limited sampling).
Leisure wear and special beers available.
No parking except by arrangement.

THE OLD FORGE BREWERY

THE TWO SAWYERS, PETT, HASTINGS, EAST SUSSEX TN35 1HB
☎ 01424 813 030
Contact Chris Humphries
Brewery in 200 year old restored village forge. Forge, anvil and bellows all retained.
♦ Tours seven days a week for up to 20 people, including sample pint. Advance notice preferred. Brewery viewing normally 15-45 minutes depending on slide show.
For parties, fee of £12 for tour, slide show, beer tasting and three-course meal in adjacent pub.

— Tyne & Wear —

VAUX

THE BREWERY, SUNDERLAND SR1 3AN
☎ 0191 567 6277
Contact Mrs A Cubitt
Brewing has taken place on the current site since 1875. The Bottling Hall is within the shell of a former playhouse, the Avenue Theatre.
♦ Tours should be booked in advance via Mrs Cubitt (ext

374), Production Manager's secretary. Parties up to 25, in sensible footwear, are given a tour of about an hour. Free pint after in hospitality bar, the Gold Tankard, where a selection of branded merchandise and breweriana items are on sale. Brewery Tap and other pubs are close by the brewery.
No fee.
Tour times 2pm Mon, Tue, Wed; 2.30pm Thur; 10.30am Fri.

— Warwickshire —

CHURCH END BREWERY

GRIFFIN INN, CHURCH ROAD, NUNEATON ROAD, OVER WHITACRE, WARWICKSHIRE B46 2LB
☎ 01675 481 567
Contact Karl Graves or Stewart Elliott
Brewery in a 350 year old barn/coffin shop/stables at the side of the Griffin Inn, a 300 year old coaching house.
Visitors welcome Mon and Tues evenings (not during summer). Beer available at the Griffin.

— West Midlands —

BASS MITCHELLS & BUTLER

CAPE HILL, PO BOX 27, BIRMINGHAM B16 0PQ
☎ 0121 420 6525
Contact Ros Kingston
The site was bought in 1879 and has listed buildings – a mixture of old and new.
Visitor Centre takes parties of 20-40 people by appointment only. Parking available. Tour includes video, tour of brewery, sampling and lunch or supper. £7. 50 plus

VAT or £9. 50 plus VAT. T-shirts, caps, jugs, plates, glasses etc available. Tours, Mon-Fri 11.30am-2pm; Mon-Thur 7.30-10pm.

HIGHGATE BREWERY

SANDYMOUNT ROAD, WALSALL WS1 3AP
☎ 01922 644 453
Contact Rachel Smith
Traditional Victorian tower brewery untouched for 50 years, listed building, mostly original.
Visitor Centre due to open 1 May 1998, Mon-Thur 12-10pm.
No fees.
Groups should book in advance.

— Wiltshire —

BUNCES BREWERY

THE OLD MILL, NETHERAVON, SALISBURY, WILTS SP4 9QB
☎ 01980 670 631
Contact Stig Anderson
Old Mill, Grade II, originally built 1920 as a water-powered generating station to provide electricity to nearby RAF base. River runs under floor. Converted to brewery 1984.
Groups of up to 20 welcome March-Nov by prior arrangement. Tours last about an hour, followed by beer tasting. Fee £3. Sweatshirts, T-shirts, drip mats, bar towels, pumpclips and stickers available. Parking for eight cars.

MOLES BREWERY

5 MERLIN WAY, BOWERHILL, MELKSHAM, WILTS SN12 6TJ
☎ 01225 704 734
Contact Roger Catte

♦ Parties of 20-25 on Tuesday evenings, 7.30-9pm, throughout the year. Fee £5 includes samples of beer and ploughmans dinner at Brewery Tap.
No shop but promotional clothing available to order.
Paying bar at Brewery Tap.

USHERS OF TROWBRIDGE

Directors House, 68 Fore Street, Trowbridge, Wilts BA14 8JF
☎ 01225 763 171
Contact Miss S Norris
Sprawling Victorian town-centre brewery.
♦ Maximum size of parties is 25 for organisations only.
Bookings to Miss S Norris at Brewery.
Arrive 7pm at Brewery Tap for talk on brewing followed by tour. Return to Tap for more beer and buffet. Finish at 10pm.
No fee.
Entry to Brewery and Brewery Tap is free. T-shirts and branded glasses and badges are available for purchase.
Tours Tue, Wed or Thur only at 7pm, all year subject to prior bookings and excluding Bank Holidays and pre-Christmas.

WADWORTH & CO

Northgate Brewery, Devizes, Wiltshire SN10 1JW
☎ 01380 723 361
Contact J Pollock
Victorian red brick tower brewery completed in 1885.
♦ No Visitor Centre but stables open to the public from 1.30-3.30pm weekdays.
Brewery tours on two evenings a week from mid-April to mid-Oct for groups from Wadworth pubs and direct-delivered free trade customers only.
In September only, evening tours Tue and Thur for the public (20 max). Pre-book in July or August.
Fee £5 for public tours includes brewery tour, visit to stables and cooperage, two pints of beer. Fee is donated to the

Wiltshire Community Foundation.
Clothing and point-of-sale items available from Reception 8.30am-5pm weekdays.

— Yorkshire —

BLACK SHEEP BREWERY

WELLGARTH, MASHAM, RIPON, N. YORKS HG4 4EN
☎ 01765 689227
Contact: Lisa Paxton
Brewery established by Paul Theakston of the Theakston brewing dynasty in part of the defunct Lightfoot's Brewery, right next door to his old family firm (now part of the Scottish Courage brewing empire).
❦ Visitor Centre with bistro, shop and "baa..r" and "shepherded" tours (their puns). Admission free to centre; one hour pre-booked daytime tour fees £3 for adults, £2 OAPs, £1.50 children; £7.50 family rate for two adults and up to four children. Includes a small sample. Evening tour at £9.95 a head includes two pints and a meal – must book. Daytime tours seven days a week, starting 11am, 12.30, 2pm, 3pm, 4pm. Evening tours Tues-Fri and Sun. Bistro open Tues-Sun; booking advisable. Whole centre closed Mon.

CLARKS BREWERY

WESTGATE, WAKEFIELD, WEST YORKS WF2 9SW
☎ 01924 372 306
Contact Richard Munro or Vickie Lord
Brewery founded 1905.
❦ Tours by appointment only. 11am-3pm, Mon-Fri. No fee. Shop open 8am-5pm Mon-Fri, 8am-1pm Sat-Sun.

CROPTON BREWERY

Woodcroft, Cropton, nr Pickering, North Yorks YO18 8HH
☎ 01751 417 310
Contact Glyn Allen or Sandra Lee
Perched high on the edge of the North York Moors National Park, brewery is a new purpose-built plant building attractively set in landscaped gardens at the New Inn (pub with restaurant on same site).
Tours, with guide, last about an hour with a talk, walk through grounds, and sampling.
Fee £2.25 adult; £1.50 for groups of 15 or more.
Paying bar.
♥ Visitor Centre seating 50+ serves light snacks, lunches and high teas. Evening meals after 5.30pm by prior arrangement. Gift shop sells beer packs, badged glasses, gift packs, mugs, mirrors, keyrings, sweatshirts, T-shirts, polo shirts, baseball caps, teapots, jugs, toys etc. Guided walk leaflets through glorious local countryside.
Brewery and Visitor Centre opening times: 10am-2pm daily Oct-Mar; 10am-4pm daily Apr-Sep.
Guided tours on the hour. Other times and evenings by prior arrangement.
Brewery tour not suitable for wheelchair access but small children and disabled guests welcome in the Visitor Centre where there is only one step and ground floor toilets are available.
Ample parking in New Inn car park. Off-road parking for two coaches on outskirts of village, but passengers can board and alight directly outside New Inn.

THE HULL BREWERY

144-148 English Street, Hull, East Yorks HU3 2BT
☎ 01482 586 364
Contact Ann Cracknell
♥ Brewery visits for organised groups (max 13), 7pm Mon

and Tue evenings throughout the year, lasting approx 35-60 minutes. Book one month in advance. No admission charge. Parking in nearby side streets.
No Visitor Centre or museum, but voucher given for a free pint of Hull ale at the Red Lion, Clarence Street, Hull (their only pub) where a buffet is also laid on for tours.

KELHAM ISLAND

23 Alma Street, Sheffield, South Yorks S3 8SA
☎ 0114 249 4800
Contact David Wickett
♥ Visits by appointment, including a talk, last one hour.
No fee.
No shop but brewery is next to the Fat Cat pub.

LINFIT BREWERY

Sair Inn, Lane Top, Linthwaite, Huddersfield, West Yorks HD7 5SG
☎ 01484 842 370
Contact Ron or Hilary
♥ Small brewhouse can accommodate tour parties of up to 10. Large groups can be split into smaller parties. Tour lasts 20-30 minutes.
No fee.
Drinks, T-shirts and sweatshirts may be bought in the pub.
Visits at any reasonable time by previous appointment.

MALTON BREWERY

Wheelgate, Malton, North Yorks YO17 0YW
☎ 01653 697 580
Contact Cilla Parlett
Brewery in converted stable block of Suddaby's Crown Hotel, an old coaching inn on the main street of Malton.
No Visitor Centre.
♥ Pre-booked visits, weekday evenings 7-7.30pm, or

Saturday and Sunday mornings at approx 11am. Ad hoc visits for small groups subject to brew days. Tourists please ring and we'll try to fit you in!
Maximum group 15. Larger parties will be split. Those waiting can use the pub facilities and sample the beers. Tour lasts approx half an hour.
T-shirts, ties and glasses available.

ROOSTERS BREWERY

20 Claro Court Business Centre, Claro Road, Harrogate, North Yorks HG1 4BA
☎ 01423 561 861
Contact Sean Franklin
Tours for 12-20 people, booked one month in advance.
£3 including talk on brewing process, pint and sandwiches.
Tours Sat 10-12 only.

RUDGATE BREWERY

2 Centre Park, Marston Business Park, Rudgate, Tockwith, York YO5 8QF
☎ 01243 358 382
Contact Richard Louden
Midweek visitors welcome at brewery.

JOHN SMITH'S

The Brewery, Tadcaster, North Yorkshire LS24 2ES
☎ 01937 832 091
Contact Nicky Richardson
Brewery built in 1890 and is a dominant feature of the small town of Tadcaster. The building is a light sandstone with the brewery tower and illuminated Magnet signs a local landmark.

❦ The museum is part of the overall tour.
Tours of 30-35. Bookings by phone or by booking form sent on request.
Tours last approx 45 minutes including museum, free bar and food.
£11.75 (£20 extra charge for less than 30 people).
Merchandise available at end of tour.
Times: 10am, 2pm, 7.30pm Mon-Fri

YORK BREWERY

12 Toft Green, Micklegate, York YO1 1JT
☎ 01904 621 162
Contact Tony Thomson
Friendly independent brewery only a few minutes walk from York's attractions, central services and amenities.
❦ Daily guided tours, including generous beer sampling: Easter-September. Mon-Sat, 11.30, 12.30, 2.30, 4pm, 6pm, 7pm; Sun 4pm, 5pm, 6pm, 7pm.
Prices £3.50 per head, £2.50 14-17 year olds and senior citizens (children welcome if well supervised).
Also do Evening Party Tours, perfect beginning to a social evening.
Brewery shop has range of high quality merchandise, polo shirts, T-shirts, pottery etc.
Brewery Tap Room with paying bar.
Regret currently not suitable for disabled visitors.

WARD'S BREWERY

Ecclesall Road, Sheffield, South Yorks S6 6NB
☎ 0114 275 5155
Contact Mr PJC Simpson (in writing only)
Brewery built 1840, still uses original tower although other buildings are more recent.
Applications in writing in advance from organised groups only.

Car parking usually available on site.
Tour not suitable for people with physical or mobility difficulties.
♥ Tours at discretion of Head Brewer twice daily Mon-Thur 2.30pm and 6.30pm, for groups of min 10, max 15 people. Last approx two hours plus approx 30 minutes in hospitality room for free sampling.
No souvenirs available.

WORTH BREWERY

Worth way, Keighley, N Yorks BD21 5LP
☎ 01535 611914
Contact: Allyson Mitchell
New brewery in big old industrial building. Comfortable Visitor Centre with bar and merchandise shop.
♥ Pre-booked tours at £3.50 a head including brewery half-pint glass and four half-pint samples. Tour lasts 90 minutes; parties of 10-52. Limited parking.
Tours 11.30am, 4pm, 7pm Mon-Thur; 11.30am and 4pm Fri, noon, 3pm, 6pm Sat.

WALES

Brains has a shop and does tours by arrangement but did not reply to our survey.

PLASSEY BREWERY

THE PLASSEY, EYTON, WREXHAM **LL13 0SP**
☎ 01978 780922
Contact Ian Dale
New brewery in old farmyard converted to crafts and shopping centre with golf course, caravan park, bistro and three bars serving Plassey ales.
♥ Pre-booked tours by arrangement; max 25; £5 per head fee includes food and samples. Shop sells beer (min quantity 10 litres) and brewery merchandise.

SCOTLAND

BORVE BREW HOUSE

RUTHVEN, BY HUNTLY, ABERDEENSHIRE **AB54 4SG**
☎ 01466 760 343
Contact James or Gregory Hughes
Brewery housed in former Victorian schoolhouse built of local granite. Original features, including cast-iron fireplace, have been retained.
♥ Visitors usually meet in bar then tour brewery in groups of less than 15. Phone first. No admission charge.

BROUGHTON ALES

BROUGHTON, BIGGAR, LANARKSHIRE **ML12 6HQ**
☎ 01899 830 345
Contact Angela Ross

♥ Tours available all year for maximum of 20 people by arrangement, usually Wed evenings 7.30-9.30.
No fee, but donation to Scottish Licensed Trade Benevolent Association appreciated. All Broughton bottled ales available plus carry-kegs and polypins.

CALEDONIAN BREWERY

42 Slateford Road, Edinburgh EH11 1PH
☎ 0131 337 1286
Contact Ron Davies
Traditional Victorian brewery (established 1869) featuring many original items. Last direct-fired open coppers in Britain. Former maltings sympathetically rebuilt after major fire in 1994.
♥ Visitor Centre in preparation. Limited disabled access and parking by arrangement. Audio-visual presentation and Internet 'virtual tour'. Evening and lunchtime functions by arrangement. Beer festivals.
Tour and tasting lasts approx one hour. Booking not essential but preferred for larger parties. Phone to check admission fee.
Merchandising in Visitor Centre and by mail order. Sample cellar in brewery, also Caley Sample Room 400m from brewery.
Visits all year except Christmas and New Year. Mon-Fri, hourly. Lunch, evening and weekends for larger parties by arrangement.

CARLSBERG-TETLEY ALLOA BREWERY

Whins Road, Alloa FK10 3RB
☎ 01259 726 000
Brewery dates back to 1810. Present brewhouse plant has the distinction of being the last cargo to arrive at Alloa docks. The vessels are all copper and form one of the most attractive brewhouses in the country.
♥ Tours only available to clubs and societies or university groups with a particular interest in the brewing industry.

THE FYFE BREWING COMPANY

469 High Street, Kirkcaldy, Fife
☎ 01592 646 211 (brewery); 01592 264 270 (bar)
Contact Nick Bromfield
Brewery in old sailmaking shed above and behind the Harbour Bar.
Small parties (max 12), duration 10-15 minutes, at any time by arrangement.
T-shirts, glasses available in Harbour Bar.

ISLE OF SKYE BREWING COMPANY

The Pier, Uig, Isle of Skye IV51 9XY
☎ 01470 542 477
Contact Angus MacRuary
Purpose-built brewery on shore of Uig Bay. No Visitor Centre but small exhibition/display incorporated into shop.
Organised tours (max 12) twice daily in season. Parties by arrangement at other times.
Fee £2 including one pint in sampling area.
Shop stocks bottled beers (Scottish), country wines and island-connected whisky. Also miscellaneous merchandise – sweatshirts, T-shirts, glasses, pens, pottery etc.
No paying bar.
Tours 1 May-30 Sept, noon and 3pm seven days a week. Other times by arrangement (please telephone).

MACLAY & CO

Thistle Brewery, Alloa, Clackmannanshire FK10 1ED
☎ 01259 723 387
Contact Roger Ryman or Duncan Kellock
Victorian tower brewery built in 1871, virtually unchanged and still using direct-fired coppers. The only Scottish brewery to use borehole water drawn from its own wells.

♦ Visitors may phone to organise tours on an ad-hoc basis. No charge. Max 12 people. Tour lasts 30 minutes to one hour depending on needs.
Free beer sampling at end of tour.
Tours preferably afternoon or early evening. CAMRA regional groups please give as much notice as possible

ORKNEY BREWERY

Quoyloo, Sandwick, Orkney, KW16 3LT
☎ 01856 841 802
Britain's most northerly brewery set amidst rolling countryside.
♦ Small Sample Bar, max 20 unless by prior arrangement.
Fee £1 for tour of brewery plus half pint of beer.
Tours 1 Apr-31 Oct, Tue-Thur at 3pm prompt.

TRAQUAIR HOUSE BREWERY

Traquair, Inverleithen, Peebles EH44 6PW
☎ 01896 830 323
Contact Catherine Maxwell Stuart
Working 18th-century brewery in spectacular 1,000 year old Scottish castle; pioneered the revival of country house brewing.
♦ Brewery can be seen as part of house tour – admission £1.50 (adults), £1 (children).
Shop sells bottled beer, glasses, other merchandise.

BUSHY'S

MOUNT MURRAY BREWERY, NEW CASTLETOWN ROAD, BRADDAN, IOM
☎ 01624 661 244
Contact Curly
Located in converted farm buildings, set in a rural valley, it has quaint visual appeal. The Bushy's mobile pub – a converted Atlantean double-decker bus – is on show under the Dutch barn.
Casual visitors are welcome but sampling beer cannot always be guaranteed. Best to phone. For organised groups, booking is a must. The sampling room is full of artefacts relating to the Isle of Man Pure Beer Laws. Packages which include the tour and a supper at one of Bushy's outlets are very popular at an inclusive price of £6.
Parties of 12-50 in size. Tour lasts between 1-3 hours depending upon interest or thirst!
Prices £3 for basic tour plus generous sampling or £6 to include supper.
No shop but good selection of merchandise available – T-shirts, sweatshirts, caps, woolly hats, scarves, badges, posters, stickers, lighters, jackets, pumpclips, vests, glasses.
No paying bar but the Hop Garden pub is alongside.
Casual visitors welcome 9-5pm Mon-Fri (phone call advised).
Organised tours, preferably Mon-Thur evenings, hours to suit.

OKELLS BREWERY

KEWAIGUE, DOUGLAS, ISLE OF MAN
☎ 01624 661 120
Contact M Cowbourne
Brand-new purpose-built brewery.

❦ Reception room. Twenty people max, normally evenings by appointment. Tour lasts 30 minutes followed by free samples.

Channel Islands

JERSEY BREWERY

57 ANN STREET, ST HELIER, JERSEY
☎ 01534 507 971
❦ Tours lasting one hour for 12 people at a time.
No fee.
No shop but gifts can be bought (towels, glasses etc).
Tours all year.

RW RANDALL

ST JULIENS AVENUE, ST PETER PORT, GUERNSEY GY1 3JG
☎ 01481 720 134
Contact Brian Randall
Old-established family-owned brewery with small museum.
❦ Brewery tours Thursdays at 2.30pm, 1 May-2 Oct. Other dates by appointment. Tour lasts 20 minutes. Max 20 people.
T-shirts, pens etc available.

– INDEX BY BREWERY –

The CAMRA Books range of guides helps you search out the best in beer (and cider) and brew it at home too!

Buying in the UK

All our books are available through bookshops in the UK. If you can't find a book send for a free catalogue to the CAMRA address below. CAMRA members should refer to their regular monthly newspaper *What's Brewing* for the latest details and member special offers. CAMRA books are also available by mail-order (postage free) from: CAMRA Books, 230 Hatfield Road, St Albans, Herts, AL1 4LW. Cheques made payable to CAMRA Ltd. telephone your credit card order on 01727 867201.

Buying outside the UK

CAMRA books are also sold in many book and beer outlets in the USA and other English-speaking countries. If you have trouble locating a particular book, use the details below to order by mail or fax (+44 1727 867670).

Carriage of £3.00 per book (Europe) and £6.00 per book (US, Australia, New Zealand and other overseas) is charged.

UK Booksellers

Call CAMRA Books for distribution details and book list. CAMRA Books are listed on all major CD-ROM book lists and on our Internet site: http://www.camra.org.uk

Overseas Booksellers

Call or fax CAMRA Books for details of local distributors.

Distributors are required for some English language territories. Rights enquiries (for non-English language editions) should be addressed to the managing editor.

Good Beer Guide to Prague & Czech Republic

by Graham Lees 256 pages Price: £8.99 ISBN 1-85249-122-1

A glorious guide to Czech brewing history as well as a comprehensive tour around the many breweries and beer outlets with tasting notes, maps, tourist information and language guide to make your stay complete. Covers pubs, beers, accommodation, opening times and food.

Good Beer Guide to Belgium and Holland

by Tim Webb 286 pages Price: £9.99 ISBN 1-85249-115-9

You'll find details of travel, accommodation, food, beer museums, brewery visits and festivals, as well as guides to the cafés, beer shops and warehouses you can visit. There are maps, tasting notes, beer style guide and a beers index.

Good Beer Guide to Munich and Bavaria

by Graham Lees 206 pages Price: £8.99 ISBN 1-85249-114-0

The guide tells you where to find the best beers and the many splendid bars, beer halls and gardens, and the food to match. Plus background information on breweries and the Munich Oktoberfest.

Good Beer Guide UK

edited by Jeff Evans – annual publication 546 pages Price: £10.99

Let CAMRA's Good Beer Guide lead the way to around 5,000 great pubs serving excellent ale – all researched and revised annually by CAMRA.

Guide to Real Cider

by Ted Bruning 256 pages Price: £7.99 ISBN 1-85249-117-5

This guide helps you find one of Britain's oldest, tastiest and most fascinating drinks. There are pubs and farmhouse producers from all over the country and outlets for Cider's equally drinkable cousin, Perry.

Known Gems & Hidden Treasures – A Pocket Guide to the Pubs of London

by Peter Haydon 224 pages Price: £7.99 ISBN 1-85249-118-3

If you visit London, then you need this guide to the well-known and historic pubs you must not miss, and also to the pubs which are hidden gems. Discover pubs with theatrical, sporting and historical connections.

Good Pub Food

by Susan Nowak 448 pages Price: £9.99 ISBN 1-85249-116-7

Pubs all over the UK serving traditional and exotic cuisine. A great way to discover Britain's 'locals', often run by top chefs.

Room at the Inn

by Jill Adam 242 pages Price: £8.99 ISBN 1-85249-119-1

Travellers and tourists looking for a traditional British alternative to bland impersonal hotels need look no further than this guide. Contains almost 350 inns which provide Bed and Breakfast as well as excellent real ale.

Guide to Home Brewing

Graham Wheeler 240 pages Price: £6.99 ISBN 1-85249-112-4

The definitive beginner's guide to home brewing. The principles, equipment and ingredients are explained and many recipes given.

Brew Your Own Real Ale at Home

by Graham Wheeler and Roger Protz

196 pages Price: £6.99 ISBN 1-85249-113-2

This book contains recipes which allow you to replicate some famous cask-conditioned beers or to customise brews to your own particular taste.

Brew Classic European Beers at Home

by Graham Wheeler and Roger Protz

196 pages Price: £8.99 ISBN 1-85249-117-5

Keen home brewers can now recreate some of the world's classic beers: pale ales, milds, porters, stouts, Pilsners, Alt, Kolsch, Trappist, wheat beers, sour beers, even the astonishing fruit lambics of Belgium, and many more.

INSTRUCTIONS TO YOUR BANK TO PAY DIRECT DEBITS

Please complete parts 1 to 4 to instruct your bank to make payments directly from your account.

Return the form to Campaign for Real Ale, 230 Hatfield Road, St Albans, Herts AL1 4LW.

To the Manager

1 Please write the full postal address of your bank branch in the box above.

2 Name(s) of account holder(s):

Address:

Post Code:

3 Account Number:

Banks may refuse to accept instructions to pay direct debits from some types of account.

Direct debit instructions should only be addressed to banks in the United Kingdom.

CAMRA Computer Membership No. (for office use only)

9	2	6	1	2	9

Originator's Identification No.

4 Your instructions to the bank, and signature.

- I instruct you to pay direct debits from my account at the request of Campaign for Real Ale Limited.
- The amounts are variable and are to be debited annually.
- I understand that Campaign for Real Ale Limited may change the amount only after giving me prior notice.
- PLEASE CANCEL ALL PREVIOUS STANDING ORDER INSTRUCTIONS IN FAVOUR OF CAMPAIGN FOR REAL ALE LIMITED.
- I will inform the bank in writing if I wish to cancel this instruction.
- I understand that if any direct debit is paid which breaks the terms of this instruction, the bank will make a refund.

Signature(s) Date

JOIN CAMRA

If you like good beer and good pubs you could be helping the fight to preserve, protect and promote them. CAMRA was set up in the early seventies to fight against the mass destruction of a part of Britain's heritage.

The giant brewers are still pushing through takeovers, mergers and closures of their smaller regional rivals. They are still trying to impose national brands of beer and lager on their customers whether they like it or not, and they are still closing down town and village pubs or converting them into grotesque 'theme' pubs.

CAMRA wants to see genuine free competition in the brewing industry, fair prices, and, above all, a top quality product brewed by local breweries in accordance with local tastes, and served in pubs that maintain the best features of a tradition that goes back centuries.

As a CAMRA member you will be able to enjoy generous discounts on CAMRA products and receive the highly rated monthly newspaper What's Brewing. You will be given the CAMRA members' handbook and be able to join in local social events and brewery trips.

To join, complete the form below and, if you wish, arrange for direct debit payments by filling in the form overleaf and returning it to CAMRA. To pay by credit card, contact the membership secretary on (01727) 867201.

Full membership £14; Joint (two people at the same address) membership £17; Life membership £168/£204. Student, pensioner, unemployed, disabled £8. Joint pensioners £11.

Please delete as appropriate:

I/We wish to become members of CAMRA.

I/We agree to abide by the memorandum and articles of association of the company.

I/We enclose a cheque/p.o. for £ (payable to CAMRA Ltd.)

Name(s)

Address

Signature(s)

CAMRA Ltd., 230 Hatfield Road, St Albans, Herts AL1 4LW